EXCEL BASICS
FOR
BEGINNERS

HENRY E. MEJIA

EXCEL BASICS FOR BEGINNERS

DISCLAIMER

Although the author has made every effort to ensure the information and examples in this book were correct at the press time, the author does not assume, and hereby disclaims, any liability to any party for loss, damage, or disruption caused by errors or omissions result from negligence, accident or any other cause.

DEDICATION

Dedicated to all the people who have the courage to follow their dreams, to grow, to go out of their comfort zones and to change the world for the better by performing as best as they can in their respective industries.

CONTENTS

CONTENTS

OTHER BOOKS BY THE AUTHOR

"EXCEL NINJAS" SERIES

Scan the QR Code or go to https://bit.ly/hemejia1 to learn more about "Excel Ninjas"

If you are serious about Excel, this is the series for YOU! - Aubrey

Explains everything you need to know – Lucy

Ready-to-use knowledge! – Wilfredo Contreras

"EXCEL CHAMPIONS" SERIES

Scan the QR Code or go to https://bit.ly/hemejia1 to learn more about "Excel Champions"

To the point how-to roadmap – Elias D Christakis

Excellent "Real World" Exercises – David L Gardner

Easy to Use and Well Explained - Manuela Tiefenbach

"EXCEL FOR BEGINNERS"

THE COMPLETE SERIES

Scan the QR Code or go to
https://bit.ly/hemejia1 to learn more about
"Excel for Beginners"

"EXCEL FOR _____" SERIES

(COMING SOON)

INTRODUCTION

Welcome to a new **EXCEL FOR BEGINNERS** book! The easiest, fastest and most novice-friendly way to start mastering Excel, specially created for people who is starting to interact with this awesome world of Microsoft Excel.

Because this is a SERIES of books, there might be several other of my books already published by the time you are reading this, so go ahead and get them too! This SERIES is the best Excel investment that you will ever make.

This "EXCEL FOR BEGINNERS" SERIES is all about:

- **Easy to Follow instructions and exercises**

- Simple and Easy language (no technical words)
- Step-by-Step Learning
- Learning through practice (from the very beginning)
- Making mistakes and learning from them
- Getting FAST RESULTS by mastering the most important features right away
- Straightforward and lean approach to make the best use of your time
- Fully Exercise-based (Practice makes progress)
- Becoming proficient in less than 10 hours!

When I was thinking about this series, what I wanted to create was a series of books worthy enough for you to say *"This book is easy, is understandable, it gets the things done!"*, and that's exactly what you get with all the EXCEL FOR BEGINNERS books!

That being said, I would like to summarize

the benefits you will experience by completing EXCEL BASICS FOR BEGINNERS:

- Become more productive
- Increase chances of getting a promotion and better jobs (More money!)
- Experience less workload (Excel does the heavy lifting)
- Have more free time
- Experience less stress
- Feel a sense of growth
- Expand your comfort zone
- Gain more confidence when performing your job
- Etc., etc.

So, my promise is to transfer to you the most amount of valuable experience in the least amount of time and pages (time is money, you know).

If you get better at Excel in less time, easily and without having to read gigantic amounts of pages, I can say that my mission here was completed.

Let's start right now. Welcome to your new journey.

GET YOUR 30 PRACTICE SPREADSHEETS

Before starting Chapter 1 I recommend you to get your 30 practice spreadsheets. To get them immediately just **Scan this QR Code or go directly to https://bit.ly/hemejia2 and follow the instructions**

If for any reason both the QR Code and the Link don't work, send an email to ems.online.empire@gmail.com saying **"Hello, I bought your book EXCEL BASICS FOR BEGINNERS and I need the 30 practice spreadsheets"**

I will gladly reply your email and send you the files. Now you are ready to start Chapter 1. Let's go!

CHAPTER 1
UNDERSTAND WHAT IS EXCEL AND WHY YOU NEED TO MASTER IT

WHAT IS MICROSOFT EXCEL EXACTLY?

Microsoft Excel is one of the most important and popular software used by companies and individuals on their day-to-day tasks. Because of that, any person with a high level of Excel abilities has an advantage over other people that just don't know how to use it.

Basically, the pages inside Excel are divided like a Grid and they are called **SPREADSHEETS** (More on this in the next chapter)

	A	B	C	D
1				
2				
3				
4				
5				
6				
7				
8				
9				

This grid-like pages allow people to insert gigantic amount of data, creating what we already know as **TABLES**.

With that data, you can do several tasks that are required, with the great advantage that Excel performs all the calculations for you (If you know how to give Excel the right orders).

NOTE:

The Mac version of Microsoft Excel is known as "NUMBERS", but it is not as good as Excel.

So, even if you have a Mac, I highly suggest that you get "Excel for Mac", not Numbers.

WHAT IS MICROSOFT EXCEL NOT SUITABLE FOR?

As you may see, grid-like pages are not suitable for long pieces of TEXT.

You can change the size of each CELL (each rectangle inside the grid is called CELL), but Microsoft Excel it is definitely not suitable for long text.

What I mean by long pieces of text is:

- All kinds of letters
- Books or Booklets
- Meeting Minutes
- Agreements
- Business Plans
- Terms of use
- Contracts
- Memorandums
- Etc.

So, if you need to create some of the previous documents, Microsoft Word is the right choice, not Microsoft Excel.

WHAT IS MICROSOFT EXCEL MOST USED FOR?

This list might be one or the largest lists you have ever read if I hadn't cut a lot of items from it. For simplicity's sake I'm going to share some of the most common uses of Excel:

- Add
- Average
- Multiply
- Create personalized formulas and decisions
- Format tables and create databases
- Filter information
- Create Heatmaps with a set of numbers
- Create charts based on tables
- Create dynamic tables based on gigantic databases
- Find patterns inside the data
- Linear programming
- Equations
- Algebra
- Client databases
- Vendors databases
- Products databases
- Financial calculations
- Personal Finance templates

- Inventory
- Sales reports
- Costs reports
- Payroll
- Market research
- Item lists
- Budgets
- Accounting
- Forecasting
- Data Analysis
- Performance Reporting
- People management
- Money management
- Investing
- E-commerce
- Etc., Etc. Etc.

This list can go on and on, but I guess you get the point.

BUT, WHY IS EXCEL SO WIDELY USED?

Because it can perform lots of calculations **FAST, AUTOMATICALLY and WITHOUT MISTAKES** (avoiding costly human mistakes) if you know how to use excel functions correctly. That way, you become more productive and businesses become more productive also.

By inserting data in an Excel Spreadsheet (Manually or copied from another source like an ERP like SAP or Oracle), you get the RAW DATA with which Excel will perform the heavy duty for you.

Take the following simple example. If I wanted to add all those numbers in the left column, that would take 1 minute with a calculator (with some chances of making a mistake), but with Excel I just use the formula **"SUM" and I get the sum in 1 second!** (Yes, 1 second). Total sum is 51175.

Then, if I need also the average of those numbers, I simply duplicate the column (right column) and use another formula to get the average in 1 second! Average is 6397.

7084	7084
5994	5994
8198	8198
5163	5163
8107	8107
8251	8251
2259	2259
6119	6119
51175	**6397**

If you need to present something visual, you can add some icons automatically just with some clicks.

✔	7084
⚠	5994
✔	8198
⚠	5163
✔	8107
✔	8251
✖	2259
⚠	6119

Do you want to organize the numbers from the largest to the smallest? 3 seconds and you have them.

✔	8251
✔	8198
✔	8107
✔	7084
!	6119
!	5994
!	5163
✖	2259

Do you need a Chart with the same numbers? 5 seconds and you get it.

And we are just scratching the surface here. Excel presents a vast world of possibilities for you!

QUICK CHAPTER SUMMARY

- Excel is a group of spreadsheets that allow you to perform complex calculations and tasks
- Excel is widely used by companies and individuals
- Excel is not suitable for large pieces of text
- Excel perform the calculations automatically as long as you know how to use Excel correctly

CHAPTER 2
START USING EXCEL RIGHT NOW

Within this brief chapter you are going to Create, Save, Duplicate and Open a spreadsheet (Remember that we call **Spreadsheets** to the Excel files).

By the way, this chapter is for people who have never used Excel, so if you already know how to create, save and open an Excel File, you can skip this Chapter,

So, let's get this done!

CREATE A SPREADSHEET

STEP 1: Please find the Microsoft Excel icon in

your computer and click it. (By the way, it doesn't matter if you have a Mac or a PC because nowadays Excel looks almost the same in both platforms)

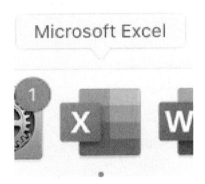

STEP 2: You'll see the following homepage (or something similar depending on your Excel version and Operating System (iOs, Windows or Linux)

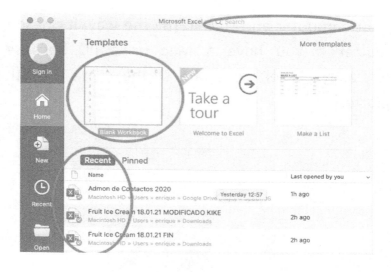

I want you to notice 3 main features:

- You will have a **SEARCH BAR**: That bar is used to search by name a spreadsheet that you have opened previously. So, to access faster to a saved file, you can try that one.

- You will have a **RECENT** list: That way you can easily open a file you opened before

- **THE MOST IMPORTANT ONE "NEW WORKBOOK"**: When you click "New Workbook" a new spreadsheet will be created. (by the way, sometimes we also call Workbook to an Excel file. So, Workbook or Spreadsheet are the same)

Go ahead and double Click **NEW WORKBOOK**!

STEP 3: Those little rectangles in all the sheet are called **CELLS**. Now that you have your Workbook, I want you click on cell **B2** and write you name inside that cell (More on cells later)

	A	B
1		
2		Henry
3		
4		

It is called B2 because it's Column B and Row 2.

Think of it as a chess table.

CONGRATULATIONS! You have CREATED a Spreadsheet! It may seem simple, but it is progress!

Now let's **SAVE** your progress!

SAVE A SPREADSHEET

To SAVE your progress I'll introduce you to one of the most important icons in Excel! The **SAVE icon**! This icon is at the TOP LEFT of your Excel Workbook.

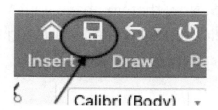

First, let me explain how it works. **It works in 2 ways:**

- If you click it for the first time with that worksheet (I mean, when you have not saved your progress before, when your worksheet is recently created) then you are going to be presented with the option to give the worksheet a **NEW NAME** (This process is called **"SAVE AS"**).

- If you click the SAVE icon AFTER you have NAMED your worksheet, all you are going to do is to save your progress. Think of this as if you were updating your file, by saving the new changes you made since the last time you clicked that icon.

IMPORTANT NOTE: It is important to SAVE as frequently as possible. You don't know when you are going to have any kind of trouble and lose all your unsaved progress.

Let's start saving your file.

STEP 1: Click the save icon for the first time and you will get a window similar to this one.

STEP 2: Change the name Book1 to **"My name"**, select "Desktop and click SAVE.

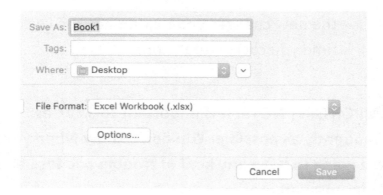

Notice the following:

- The words **"Save As"** appear next to **"Book1".** It is in that box where you can NAME your file however you want.
- The next important field is **"Where"**, so you have to choose the location you want to save your file. Just for this time, please just name your file **"My name"**.
- The file format is going to be **"Excel Workbook (.xlsx)**
- Then click **"SAVE"**

The you have it. Your file is in your desktop.

STEP 3: Write something else in the next cell, anything.

STEP 4: Click the save button again to save your progress (The new "something" you wrote in STEP 3.

That way you save your progress.

IMPORTANT: Remember to ALWAYS constantly save your progress

OPEN AN EXISITNG SPREADSHEET

This part is so easy, we will get through this fast. To open an existing Spreadsheet, I'm going to ask you to close your Spreadsheet called "My Name" first.

STEP 1: Close your spreadsheet called "My name"

STEP 2: Go to your desktop where you saved your file.

STEP 3: Double click that same file

STEP 4: Voila! The same file is open

Although this was very simple, now let's DUPLICATE THAT SAME FILE, but with another name (That's why is called to duplicate)

DUPLICATE AN EXISITNG SPREADSHEET

In order to DUPLICATE an existing spreadsheet is necessary to:

1. Have previously saved the spreadsheet we are going to duplicate.

2. Open the file

3. Use the feature **SAVE AS** to save the file with another name

So, let's do it

STEP 1: With the file "My name" open, go to the top left of your screen, Click **FILE** and then click **SAVE AS**

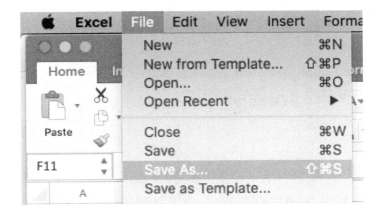

STEP 2: Write ANOTHER NAME ("Duplicated File" as an example) and choose the location (you can use Desktop) and Click **SAVE.**

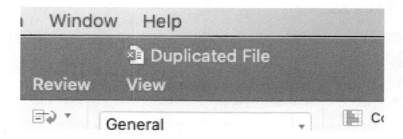

STEP 3: Confirm that you have done thing correctly by looking at the top part of your Excel spreadsheet. It must have the new name.

STEP 4: If you go to your desktop, you will notice that you have both files, My Name and Duplicated File.

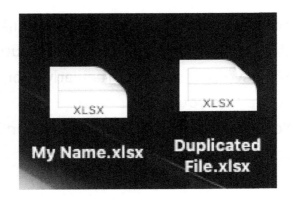

WHY IS DUPLICATING IMPORTANT?

When you want to make some changes to a file, but you still want to keep your actual file as a backup file, you will need to duplicate the file BEFORE you start making those changes.

If something wrong happens and you screw it up, you can go back to your backup file, duplicate it again and start over.

CONGRATULATIONS! You have completed this basic introductory tutorial. Now, let's start the real training.

QUICK CHAPTER SUMMARY:

- To create, open, save and duplicate files is the very foundation of your Excel journey.
- You save your progress regularly in order not to lose your work.
- You duplicate your file when you want to create a backup file.

CHAPTER 3
UNDERSTAND EXCEL BASIC PARTS

Within this chapter you are going to get familiar with the Excel layout. The goal in this chapter is that you understand the basic definitions in order for you to get a solid foundation for the next chapter.

To better understand this, I've created an exercise spreadsheet so, let's go!

LET'S SOLVE AN EXERCISE!

Open file ExcelBasicsChapter3ex1.xlsx

Within this exercise, our main goal is to understand the main parts of Excel and how they relate.

When you open your file, you will see something like this

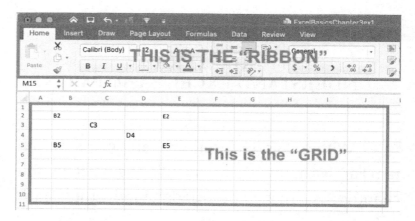

So, the first thing you need to understand is that you will see 2 main parts (you have more of them, but to keep this simple let's focus on this two)

THE GRID

The grid is the sheet itself, is where you write or paste your data and where you perform the modifications that you need.

As you may see, the GRID has COLUMNS and ROWS. The Columns are named A, B, C, E, etc., and the ROWS are named 1, 2, 3, 4, etc., creating something like a giant chessboard.

The CELLS (squares or rectangles of the grid) are named with the letter and number from the COLUMN and ROW they belong to. So, to give you an example, I wrote B2 (the name of the cell) in that exact cell.

Let's modify that

EXERCISE STEP 1: By clicking in the cell, write the correct name in the correct cell according to this list:

B2 Brad Pitt

C3 Nicolas Cage

D4 Tom Cruise

E5 Gal Gadot

Your Spreadsheet must look like this!

▲	A	B	C	D	E
1					
2	BRAD PITT			E2	
3			NICOLAS CAGE		
4				TOM CRUISE	
5		B5			GAL GADOT

Now, when I say "Look at cell G8" or "Position yourself on cell D20", you will know what I'm talking about!

THE RIBBON

The ribbon is much more complex than the grid because it has so many features, but don't freak out. In order to navigate throughout this book and keep it as useful and as easy as possible, we are going to focus in the most important features, the ones that give you the most value.

The Ribbon is divided in 2 sections: The Tabs section and the Features section.

The TABS are: Home, Draw, Page layout, Formulas, Data, Review and View.

The FEATURES are different for each TAB!

Look at the picture above, that is the HOME Tab and those are the Features of the HOME TAB.

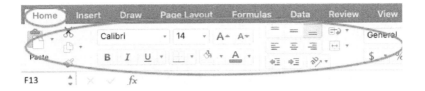

EXERCISE STEP 2: Now, please click the "FORMULAS TAB" and look at the following picture, this is the FORMULAS Tab and those are the FEATURES for the FORMULAS Tab. (That way you are learning to go back and forth with the TABS)

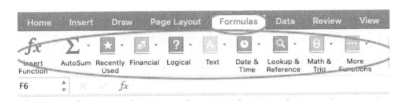

Just keep in mind that we are going to learn this stuff later in the book.

THE SHEETS

Please look at the bottom-left part of your

Excel and you'll find this

Those are the SHEETS of the entire WORKBOOK (or entire SPREADSHEET).

And what does that mean? It means that you can have several Sheets INSIDE the same workbook. Let's take this example: **If the WORKBOOK is called "SALES OF COMPANY ABC", it is possible that the Workbook has some SHEETS called: Sales executives, Products, Inventory, Performance, etc.**

Due to the convenience, you can gather different sheets that are needed in order to complete the main purpose of the WORKBOOK you created.

EXERCISE STEP 3: Please Go to Sheet 2 (by clicking on Sheet 2) and write your name those 4 times, then go back to Sheet 1 (That way, you are learning how to go back and forth inside your worksheet)

YOUR NAME HERE

YOUR NAME HERE

YOUR NAME HERE

YOUR NAME HERE

THE ZOOM SECTION

Please look at the bottom-right part of your Excel and you'll find this

This one is simple enough. With this tool, you enlarge the Grid or you make it smaller WITHOUT having to increase the font size in the document. In other words, this increases the view of the whole sheet.

Try it out, increase to 150% by clicking the plus sign. Then decrease it again to 100%.

CONGRATULATIONS! That's it for this chapter. This one was easy. In the next chapter you are going to start having lots of exercises to solve!

QUICK CHAPTER SUMMARY:

- The main parts of the Excel display are the Grid and the Ribbon
- The Ribbon has 2 parts: Tabs and Features
- Also, you have Sheets and Zoom

CHAPTER 4
START USING BASIC FORMATTING AND EDITING

Within this chapter you are going to learn how to use the most important and basic Excel features in order to start working right away.

This is where your productivity will start to increase a little bit, simply because you will learn the 20% most important features that deliver 80% of the results!

Also, in this chapter you will start to get more serious homework! We will solve some exercises together but you need to promise to solve the homework exercises also.

LET'S SOLVE AN EXERCISE!

Open file ExcelBasicsChapter4ex1.xlsx

Within this exercise, our main goal is to learn to use the RIBBON a little bit in order to format and modify the information that is already inside the spreadsheet.

When you open your spreadsheet, you will find the following data:

CHRIS EVANS	BRAD PITT	JAMIE FOXX	IDRIS ELBA
ROBERT DOWNEY JR	MATT DAMON	EMMA STONE	TOM HANKS
JENNIFER LAWRENCE	WILL SMITH	NICOLAS CAGE	CARA DELEVINGNE
CHANNING TATUM	PAUL RUDD	TOM CRUISE	WILL FERRELL
GEORGE CLOONEY	BEN AFFLECK	CHRIS PRATT	BEN STILLER
JOHNNY DEPP	MATTHEW MCCONAUGHEY	SAMUEL L. JACKSON	MELISSA MCCARTHY
MARGOT ROBBIE	TOM HARDY	LEONARDO DICAPRIO	VIN DIESEL
RYAN REYNOLDS	CHRIS HEMSWORTH	TOM HOLLAND	CHARLIZE THERON
RYAN GOSLING	TOM HIDDLESTON	TYLER PERRY	ANNA KENDRICK

SCARLETT
JOHANSSON   DWAYNE JOHNSON   GAL GADOT

BRADLEY
COOPER

Yes, those are famous actors and actresses!
We are going to use them in all our exercises to
make them interesting!

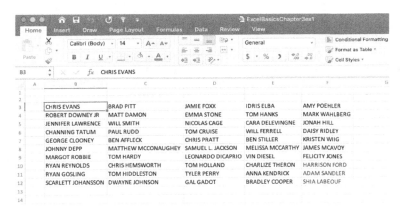

IMPORTANT NOTE:

**If you want to search for a word or a name inside
the whole sheet, you can use the "SEARCH
SHEET" feature on the Top Right of your screen**

**If you write something, it will find it and highlight
the cell in which it is found. Also, you get the**

chance to find several cells that have the same word or name by clicking the right and left arrows that appear there.

It is time to use the features of the HOME tab!

STEP 1: If you are not there, please click the **HOME** tab (upper left part of your screen)

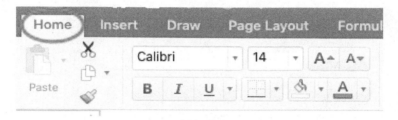

In the previous image, notice that you have lots of different buttons. We will skip some of them and we will learn the most useful ones.

STEP 2: Let's start with the FONT COLOR. Please, position yourself in C3 (Brad Pitt) and change the color of the font by clicking the little arrow of this button

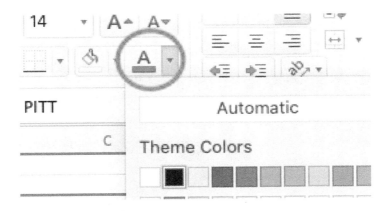

Change the color to GREEN!

CHRIS EVANS   BRAD PITT   JAMIE FOXX

ROBERT DOWNEY JR   MATT DAMON   EMMA STONE

That's it! That is how you change the font color

STEP 3: Now, let's change the BACKGROUND COLOR. Position yourself in B4 (Robert Downey Jr) and click the little arrow next to the BUCKET button, and change the background color to yellow.

Now you have something like this

CHRIS EVANS BRAD PITT

ROBERT DOWNEY JR MATT DAMON

JENNIFER LAWRENCE WILL SMITH

STEP 4: Now, let's change the FONT STYLE, you can choose between BOLD, ITALIC or UNDERLINED.

Please make Jennifer Lawrence BOLD, Will Smith ITALIC and Nicolas Cage UNDERLINED.

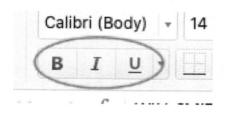

Just select Jennifer Lawrence and then click the B to make it BOLD. Then repeat the same process with the other guys

JENNIFER   *WILL*   <u>NICOLAS</u>
LAWRENCE   *SMITH*   <u>CAGE</u>

STEP 5: The next step is to change the FONT itself and the SIZE of the font. To do that you need to use these 2 parts.

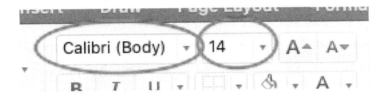

Please, position yourself is C5 (Ben Affleck) and change the FONT by clicking the little arrow to the right of the actual font name (Select the font you want). And then, change the size to 20!

Look how it looks different!

NOTE: By the way, the 2 buttons with an A to the right of the size button are also used to change size, but the increase or decrease the size by one step at a time.

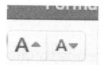

STEP 6: The next step is to ALIGN the text inside each cell. I will ask you to select the from C3 to C12 (just click on C3 and DRAG the mouse to C12 WITHOUT releasing the click) and ALIGN all of them to the center of each cell by clicking this button.

Look how all the names in that column are now centered.

BRAD PITT

MATT DAMON

WILL SMITH

PAUL RUDD

BEN AFFLECK

MATTHEW MCCONAUGHEY

TOM HARDY

CHRIS HEMSWORTH

TOM HIDDLESTON

DWAYNE JOHNSON

STEP 7: ALIGN to the RIGHT the D Column (From Jamie Foxx to Gal Gadot) by following the same process but using this button instead.

JAMIE FOXX

EMMA STONE

NICOLAS CAGE

TOM CRUISE

CHRIS PRATT

SAMUEL L. JACKSON

LEONARDO
DICAPRIO

TOM HOLLAND

TYLER PERRY

GAL GADOT

STEP 8: Lastly, apply the same formatting to an entire column (COPY AND PASTE THE FORMATTING). To do that, I'm going to ask you to take Scarlett Johansson as a guinea pig and format her in every possible way: Background, Font color, Font style, Font size, alignment, etc.

This is my example

Once you have done that, you are going to COPY THE FORMATTING AND APPLY IT TO THE ENTIRE E COLUMN. (From Idris Elba to Bradley Cooper). But how?

With this small BRUSH BUTTON here.

First, select Scarlett Johansson, then click the brush button once, then select from Idris Elba to Bradley Cooper WITHOUT RELEASING THE CLICK! And there you have it! Everything is formatted the same as Scarlett Johansson!

IDRIS ELBA

TOM HANKS

CARA DELEVINGNE

WILL FERRELL

BEN STILLER

MELISSA MCCARTHY

VIN DIESEL

CHARLIZE THERON

ANNA KENDRICK

BRADLEY COOPER

This tool is very useful when you need to format lots of cells the same way.

IMPORTANT NOTE:

You can change the size of the columns and the rows by clicking between the letters and numbers and dragging the line.

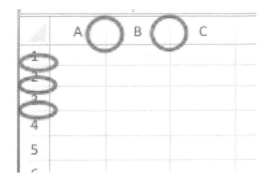

By clicking in the middle of A and B and dragging the mouse to the right, you can increase the width of A Column. By clicking in the middle of B and C and dragging the mouse to the right, you can increase the width of B Column.

Also, by clicking in the middle of 1 and 2 and dragging the mouse down, you can increase the height of Row 1. By clicking in the middle of 2 and 3 and dragging the mouse down, you can increase the height of Row 3.

CONGRATULATIONS! This was it with the basic formatting chapter. I would love to spend more time with other basic formatting features, but we still have a long way to go with other more important features ahead! So, let's continue

By the way, I told you that you would have homework to do, so here it is.

MORE EXERCISES:

- ExcelBasicsChapter4ex2.xlsx
- ExcelBasicsChapter4ex3.xlsx
- ExcelBasicsChapter4ex4.xlsx
- ExcelBasicsChapter4ex5.xlsx
- ExcelBasicsChapter4ex6.xlsx

QUICK CHAPTER SUMMARY:

- Basic Formatting is one of the first thing you need to learn in order to become a great Excel User

- You can use the Search Sheet to easily find words inside the sheet
- There are lots of formatting features, but the ones that we learned in this chapter are the most important
- 80% of the time, these basic formatting features are going to be enough!
- You can change the size of the columns and rows

Are you enjoying this book?

Do you think it's easy to understand?

Have the exercises helped you learn faster?

Without knowing your opinion, I won't know if the book has helped you to become a better Excel user.

You can share your thoughts with me by writing a Review

CHAPTER 5
KNOW AND UNDERSTAND THE BASIC
RIGHT CLICK FEATURES

This is a brief chapter and you will probably think it is a little bit unnecessary, but I'm just making sure that you dominate these little things before moving forward to one of the most important topics of the book, Excel Formulas!

So, withing this chapter you are going to learn to Copy, Paste and Cut cells! Also, you'll learn additional formatting features.

Let's begin the exercise right now.

Open file ExcelBasicsChapter5ex1.xlsx

When you open the file, you'll find 2 tables

TEAM 1	SALARY	%			
CHRIS EVANS	462228		*IDRIS ELBA*	*208685*	
ROBERT DOWNEY JR	*285800*		*TOM HANKS*	*199206*	
JENNIFER LAWRENCE	124621		*CARA DELEVINGNE*	*435930*	
CHANNING TATUM	433881		*WILL FERRELL*	*123369*	
GEORGE CLOONEY	*317886*		BEN STILLER	258952	
JOHNNY DEPP	269690		*MELISSA MCCARTHY*	*263828*	
MARGOT ROBBIE	483213		*VIN DIESEL*	*170638*	
RYAN REYNOLDS	139512		CHARLIZE THERON	442507	
RYAN GOSLING	217435		*ANNA KENDRICK*	*118410*	
SCARLETT JOHANSSON	210118		*BRADLEY COOPER*	*175465*	

Notice that you have 2 columns with names

and their corresponding salary. But also notice that some names are formatted (Bold, italic, underlined and with background color) and some of them are not. That is because they belong to different teams (Team 1 to the left and Team 2 to the right)

Our job is to use create the top row for Team 2, and then we need to move the names that belong to the other team WITHOUT MESSING THE TABLES UP!

COPYING AND PASTING

STEP 1: Let's create the Top Row of Team #2. To do that, you need to COPY the following 3 cells: B2, C2 and D2.

TEAM 1	SALARY	%

Just for you to practice, let's do this ONE by ONE starting with D2. Please Click **WITH THE RIGHT BUTTON OF YOUR MOUSE** the cell D2 (%) and select "**COPY**"

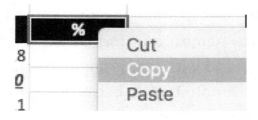

STEP 2: After clicking "Copy", go to cell H2, RIGHT CLICK and select PASTE

There you have it, that is the first part, but I'm going to show you a little trick (a widely known keyboard shortcut)

STEP 3: Let's do the same with the word SALARY in C2, but this time you are NOT going to use the right click, you are going to Press **CTRL+C** (or **COMMAND+C** if you are using a Mac) in your keyboard.

Remember, you need to first press CTRL, hold it and press C WITHOUTH RELEASING CONTROL. Once you have done this, you can release both keys.

NOTE:

CTRL+C and COMMAND+C are the fast way to COPY a cell. That way you are able to copy any cell or cells that you are currently selecting.

STEP 4: Go to cell G2 and PASTE it by using **CTRL+V** or **COMMAND+V**. That one is the keyboard shortcut to PASTE

STEP 5: Repeat the process to copy B2 (Team 1) into cell F2. But, in order to change the name to "Team 2", just DOUBLE CLICK the cell, erase the number 1 and write the number 2. That is how you edit the text inside a cell without erasing the complete cell.

What you need to remember about copying and pasting is that you are DUPLICATING a cell by copying it and paste the same info in another cell.

Next, you are going to CUT and PASTE, which is a little bit different because when you CUT you DO NOT duplicate, instead you REMOVE the first cell and PLACE it in another cell.

CUTING AND PASTING

Now is time to reorganize the Team members and their salaries (Yes, obviously the salary goes with them). You need to move Robert Downey and George Clooney from Team 1 to Team 2. Also, you need to move Ben Stiller and Charlize Theron from Team 2 to Team 1.

TEAM 1	SALARY	%	TEAM 2	SALARY	%
CHRIS EVANS	462228		*IDRIS ELBA*	*208685*	
ROBERT DOWNEY JR	*285800*		*TOM HANKS*	*199206*	
JENNIFER LAWRENCE	124621		*CARA DELEVINGNE*	*435930*	
CHANNING TATUM	433881		*WILL FERRELL*	*123369*	
GEORGE CLOONEY	*317886*		BEN STILLER	258952	

JOHNNY DEPP	269690	*MELISSA MCCARTHY*	*263828*
MARGOT ROBBIE	483213	*VIN DIESEL*	*170638*
RYAN REYNOLDS	139512	CHARLIZE THERON	442507
RYAN GOSLING	217435	*ANNA KENDRICK*	*118410*
SCARLETT JOHANSSON	210118	*BRADLEY COOPER*	*175465*

The most efficient way to do it is by CUTTING and PASTING.

STEP 1: Select Robert Downey Jr and his salary (B4 and C4), the RIGHT CLICK them and click CUT

CHRIS EVANS	402228	
ROBERT DOWNEY JR	28580(	Cut
JENNIFER LAWRENCE	12462	Copy
CHANNING TATUM	43388	Paste
GEORGE CLOONEY	317001	

STEP 2: Once you have done that you will need to find 2 cells to "temporarily deposit" Robert Downey and his salary and paste them there.

You can Paste them in B15 and C15. Go ahead, RIGHT CLICK cell B15 and select PASTE

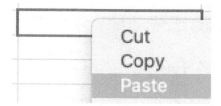

Voila! Robert Downey disappeared from the table and now is outside it. Also notice that even though you just right clicked B15 to paste Robert Downey, Excel also pasted his salary because you have previously cut it along with the name.

TEAM 1	SALARY	%
CHRIS EVANS	462228	
JENNIFER LAWRENCE	124621	
CHANNING TATUM	433881	
GEORGE CLOONEY	*317886*	
JOHNNY DEPP	269690	
MARGOT ROBBIE	483213	
RYAN REYNOLDS	139512	
RYAN GOSLING	217435	

SCARLETT JOHANSSON   210118

ROBERT DOWNEY JR   285800

STEP 3: Now let's try the keyboard shortcut to CUT (CTRL+X for Windows and COMMAND+X for Mac).

Please cut George Clooney and his salary by using the keyboard shortcut. Remember that you need to click CTRL, hold it and click X without releasing CTRL. After that, you can release both keys.

STEP 4: Now "deposit" George Clooney anywhere (B17 is a good choice) by using the PASTE shortcut CTRL+V for Windows and COMMAND+V for Mac).

TEAM 1	SALARY	%
CHRIS EVANS	462228	
JENNIFER LAWRENCE	124621	
CHANNING TATUM	433881	

JOHNNY DEPP	269690
MARGOT ROBBIE	483213
RYAN REYNOLDS	139512
RYAN GOSLING	217435
SCARLETT JOHANSSON	210118

Now, both are outside the table, but they are still there in the spreadsheet. The next step is to **Cut and Paste** Ben Stiller and Charlize Theron from Team 2 to Team 1, inside the empty cells, and then move Robert and George to Team 2

STEP 5: You already know how to do this. Just use the shortcuts or the mouse to cut and paste the names in the correct teams.

TEAM 1	SALARY	%	TEAM 2	SALARY	%
CHRIS EVANS	462228		*IDRIS ELBA*	*208685*	
BEN STILLER	258952		*TOM HANKS*	*199206*	
JENNIFER LAWRENCE	124621		*CARA DELEVINGNE*	*435930*	
CHANNING	433881		*WILL FERRELL*	*123369*	

TATUM

CHARLIZE THERON	442507	*ROBERT DOWNEY JR*	*285800*
JOHNNY DEPP	269690	*MELISSA MCCARTHY*	*263828*
MARGOT ROBBIE	483213	*VIN DIESEL*	*170638*
RYAN REYNOLDS	139512	*GEORGE CLOONEY*	*317886*
RYAN GOSLING	217435	*ANNA KENDRICK*	*118410*
SCARLETT JOHANSSON	210118	*BRADLEY COOPER*	*175465*

Great! That is how you use COPY, CUT and PASTE! There is no way to use Excel without knowing these shortcuts!

NUMBERS FORMATTING

To format the salary as CURRENCY or MONEY, just select all the cells you want to format, go to HOME TAB, and find this button.

That way you will have the numbers formatted as currency.

TEAM 2	SALARY
IDRIS ELBA	$ 208,685.00
TOM HANKS	$ 199,206.00
CARA DELEVINGNE	$ 435,930.00
WILL FERRELL	$ 123,369.00

Do you want to remove the decimals? Just use these 2 buttons to add or remove the decimals

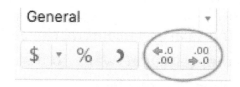

TEAM 2	SALARY
IDRIS ELBA	*$ 208,685*
TOM HANKS	*$ 199,206*
CARA DELEVINGNE	*$ 435,930*
WILL FERRELL	*$ 123,369*

That's it for this brief chapter! I told you it was easy. The real challenge begins in the following chapter!

MORE EXERCISES:

- ExcelBasicsChapter5ex2.xlsx
- ExcelBasicsChapter5ex3.xlsx

QUICK CHAPTER SUMMARY:

- Copy and Paste is the most used set of shortcuts.
- Cut and Paste is another useful shortcut

- Basically, those are used to "duplicate" or to "move" information from one cell to another.
- Currency formatting is always handy because you'll almost always work with money figures at Excel

CHAPTER 6
LEARN AND USE THE TOP 4 FORMULAS

Here we are! The Formulas Chapter. I'm so excited because formulas are one of the main tools inside Excel. In fact, you can't say that you are an Excel user if you don't know how to use several formulas correctly.

Let's start from the very beginning and then let's build up from there.

WHAT IS A FORMULA?

A Formula (sometimes also called Function) is an order you give to Excel, and in return, Excel performs that action every time the situation is appropriate. That was the simplest way to explain what a formula is.

Let's suppose that you have the following table and you want to get to TOTAL SUM of the monthly earnings

	MONTHLY EARNINGS
AMY POEHLER	$ 51,680
MARK WAHLBERG	$ 85,565
JONAH HILL	$ 57,273
DAISY RIDLEY	$ 71,007
KRISTEN WIIG	$ 79,656

To do that, you would need to write the formula *=SUM(C3:C12)* at the bottom of the earnings (More on how to create formulas later on this chapter).

If you sum (by hand) all of the previous earnings, you will get the total amount of **$345,181**. Amount that I got is 3 seconds using my formula

MONTHLY EARNINGS

AMY POEHLER	$	51,680
MARK WAHLBERG	$	85,565
JONAH HILL	$	57,273
DAISY RIDLEY	$	71,007
KRISTEN WIIG	$	79,656
	$	**345,181**

What if want the average DIRECTLY? (without having to sum and then divide) There is another formula for that, called AVERAGE

MONTHLY EARNINGS

AMY POEHLER	$	51,680
MARK WAHLBERG	$	85,565
JONAH HILL	$	57,273
DAISY RIDLEY	$	71,007
KRISTEN WIIG	$	79,656

$ 69,036

This is kind of easy with 5 employees, maybe you were used to do it by hand. But when you have hundreds of entries, you will need the formulas!

HOW MANY FORMULAS ARE THERE?

There are lots of them and in this book, you are going to learn the most basic and useful ones! If you want to dive deeper (and you should), I highly suggest that you get my other books that specialize in Excel Formulas

HOW DO YOU WRITE FORMULAS?

The simplest form to create a formula is to go to the cell where you want it and start with an EQUAL sign = followed by the name of the formula and then the structure of the formula.

IMPORTANT:

To tell Excel that you want to write a formula, you need to start by writing =

The next most important thing you need to keep in mind when talking about formulas is the STRUCTURE or the formula.

We call STRUCTURE to the formula parts that are needed. It follows this layout always:

=NAMEOFTHEFORMULA(argument1, argument 2, etc)

What does that mean?

- **Equal sign (=)** is the way you start creating a formula. Basically, when you need a formula the first thing you need to do in the cell is to write the equal sign. That way Excel knows that you want to create a formula.

- **NAMEOFTHEFORMULA** is where you write the name of the specific formula you want to create. Remember that there are more than 100 formulas you can use, and each one of them has its own name. This is how you tell excel which formula you want to use.

- **Arguments** are the "variables" of the formula. In simple words, the arguments are the specific data and commands you are giving Excel. Normally, those arguments are groups of cells. We will discuss this in the first exercise of this chapter.

With that, you are able to create powerful and specific formulas that do the heavy lifting for you!

And because I think that the best way to learn something is by doing it, let' start with some exercises, you'll understand this better when we have solved some of them together!

THE TOP 4 FORMULAS YOU NEED TO USE!

These are the Top 4 Formulas you are going to use and the ones that we are going to practice right now:

- SUM

- AVERAGE
- VLOOKUP (The most powerful search formula)
- IF (The most powerful logical formula)

So, without saying anything else, let's start with the exercises

SUM FORMULA

Open file ExcelBasicsChapter6ex1.xlsx

In this exercise you will find a table with the investment income of each of our Hollywood stars. Also, the income is shown by month of the first quarter of the year.

Your job is to find the total earnings PER MONTH and also PER ACTOR or ACTRESS. To do that, you will need to use the formula **SUM.**

NAME	JAN	FEB	MAR
CHRIS EVANS	$ 9,473	$ 5,858	$ 5,951
ROBERT DOWNEY JR	$ 8,614	$ 9,427	$ 6,278

EXCEL BASICS FOR BEGINNERS

JENNIFER LAWRENCE	$ 8,078	$ 8,554	$ 5,858
CHANNING TATUM	$ 5,973	$ 8,519	$ 5,661
GEORGE CLOONEY	$ 5,820	$ 8,373	$ 7,334
JOHNNY DEPP	$ 7,156	$ 7,318	$ 8,790

STEP 1: The first and most important step when using the SUM formula is to **FIND WHERE TO WRITE THE FORMULA** by looking at the table.

If you look at the table, you will find that the most suitable place to display the TOTAL SUM of JANUARY earnings is at cell **C18** (displayed as a green cell) which is at the bottom of the column.

Also, the most suitable cells to display the TOTAL SUM of **February and March** are **D18 and E18** accordingly.

Moreover, the best place to display the TOTAL QUATERLY earnings of **CHRIS EVANS** is **F3** (Green cell).

That said, now you know WHERE to start writing you formulas.

STEP 2: Start writing the SUM Formula. Let's start at C18 to get the TOTAL EARNINGS of JANUARY.

Position yourself at C18 and please start by writing this

=SUM

Why? Because the equal sign tells Excel that you are starting a formula and SUM is the name of the formula you want to perform.

IMPORTANT NOTE:

IF YOU ARE GETTING CERTAIN ERRORS LIKE #NAME, YOU CAN EITHER DOUBLE CLICK THE CELL OR GO DIRECTLY TO THE FORMULA BAR ON THE RIBBON TO CONTINUE MODIFYING THE FORMULA

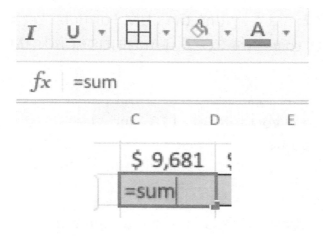

STEP 3: Continue by opening a parenthesis

=SUM(

Why? Because the parenthesis tells Excel that you are going to start writing the necessary data to perform the calculation. That data must be written INSIDE parenthesis.

STEP 4: Start including the cells you want to S You can do this in 2 different ways:

- You can either click ever cell individually,
- Or you can

What is a Range of cells? A Range of cells looks something like this:

C3:C17

It means that every cell between those cells are included in the formula (C3, C4, C5, C6, etc., until C17)

That saves lots of time, **instead of writing** **C3+C4+C5+C6** and so on.

So, let's continue. Please write that range of cells or click and drag to select those cells.

=SUM(C3:C17

$ 5,695	$ 6,
$ 6,204	$ 8,9
$ 8,439	$ 9,
$ 9,681	$ 8,
=sum(C3:C17	

STEP 5: Finally, close the parenthesis and press enter! There you have it!

=SUM(C3:C17)

WILL SMITH	$ 6,204	$ 8,985	$ 5,006
PAUL RUDD	$ 8,439	$ 9,390	$ 7,866
BEN AFFLECK	$ 9,681	$ 8,175	$ 5,552
$ 112,999			

The total investment income for our 15 Hollywood stars is $112,999 just in JANUARY

STEP 6: It is time to fill the results for **FEBRUARY and MARCH.**

To do that, you can either repeat the same process of creating the formula from scratch or click and drag the same formula you just created. (This click and drag option is easier and faster)

To drag it, just position yourself in bottom right corner of the C18 cell, click and (WITHOUT releasing the click) drag the formula to the next cell.

?	8,439	?9,390	?7,866
$ 9,681	$8,175	$5,552	
$112,999			

This process is known ad **CLICK, HOLD, AND DRAG**, and it is widely used to **REPLICATE FORMULAS** to the contiguous cells.

Once you have done that, you will notice that every single result is there, automatically and fast.

MATT DAMON	$ 5,695	$ 6,232	$ 8,177
WILL SMITH	$ 6,204	$ 8,985	$ 5,006
PAUL RUDD	$ 8,439	$ 9,390	$ 7,866
BEN AFFLECK	$ 9,681	$ 8,175	$ 5,552
	$ 112,999	$ 119,292	$ 104,013

TOTAL EARNINGS FOR FEBRUARY are $119,292

TOTAL EARNINGS FOR MARCH $104,013

Moreover, if you double click on. D18 and E18,

you'll see that the formula was AUTOMATICALLY WRITTEN AND ADAPTED FOR YOU!

39	$	9,390	$
31	$	8,175	$
99	=SUM(D3:D17)		

STEP 7: Do the same for each ACTOR. Go to F3 and write the formula to get the TOTAL QUATERLY EARNINGS FOR CHRIS EVANS:

=SUM(C3:E3)

NAME	JAN	FEB	MAR	
CHRIS EVANS	$ 9,473	$ 5,858	$ 5,951	$ 21,282
ROBERT DOWNEY JR	$ 8,614	$ 9,427	$ 6,278	

C3:E3 involves cells C3 ($9473), D3 ($5858) and E3 ($5951) so the total is $21,282

Also, **CLICK, HOLD, AND DRAG DOWN!!** In order to get all the results in less than 3 seconds!

NAME	JAN	FEB	MAR	
CHRIS EVANS	$ 9,473	$ 5,858	$ 5,951	$ 21,282
ROBERT DOWNEY JR	$ 8,614	$ 9,427	$ 6,278	$ 24,319
JENNIFER LAWRENCE	$ 8,078	$ 8,554	$ 5,858	$ 22,490
CHANNING TATUM	$ 5,973	$ 8,519	$ 5,661	$ 20,153
GEORGE CLOONEY	$ 5,820	$ 8,373	$ 7,334	$ 21,527
JOHNNY DEPP	$ 7,156	$ 7,318	$ 8,790	$ 23,264
MARGOT ROBBIE	$ 7,626	$ 9,912	$ 8,469	$ 26,007
RYAN REYNOLDS	$ 8,961	$ 7,561	$ 5,407	$ 21,929
RYAN GOSLING	$ 7,774	$ 6,453	$ 8,500	$ 22,727
SCARLETT JOHANSSON	$ 5,179	$ 5,701	$ 7,021	$ 17,901
BRAD PITT	$ 8,326	$ 8,834	$ 8,143	$ 25,303

	$	$	$	$
MATT DAMON	5,695	6,232	8,177	20,104
WILL SMITH	6,204	8,985	5,006	20,195
PAUL RUDD	8,439	9,390	7,866	25,695
BEN AFFLECK	9,681	8,175	5,552	23,408
	112,999	119,292	104,013	

Voila! There you have it! Lots of results and you just had to write 2 formulas and drag them!

CONGRATULATIONS! You now know how to use the SUM formula! Let's continue.

AVERAGE FORMULA

Now is the time for you to learn the AVERAGE formula. This exercise will be easy because we will take almost the same exercise than the previous one.

The main difference is that this time, the

table contains 6 months of earnings and that you are not trying to figure out the total sum, you are trying to figure out the AVERAGE.

JAN	FEB	MAR	APR	MAY	JUN
$ 6,421	$ 5,155	$ 7,144	$ 6,670	$ 4,731	$ 5,123
$ 8,750	$ 7,711	$ 6,686	$ 8,850	$ 3,862	$ 6,346
$ 3,160	$ 3,952	$ 4,930	$ 3,433	$ 6,160	$ 4,736
$ 3,483	$ 8,014	$ 7,096	$ 7,687	$ 7,289	$ 7,988
$ 3,180	$ 5,858	$ 6,698	$ 8,090	$ 8,542	$ 7,088

Open file ExcelBasicsChapter6ex2.xlsx

STEP 1: FIND WHERE TO WRITE THE FORMULA by looking at the table. You will notice that you have green cells in C18 and I3. You can start by writing the formula there and then drag the formula accordingly.

STEP 2: WRITE THE AVERAGE FORMULA AT C18.

Start by writing

=AVERAGE(

Remember that AVERAGE is the name of the formula, so you need to write the equal sign, the word AVERAGE and to open the parenthesis.

STEP 3: WRITE OR SELECT THE RANGE INSIDE THE PARENTHESIS.

Once you have written the formula and opened the parenthesis, you will have the option either to click, select and drag the RANGE, or to manually write it.

=AVERAGE(C3:C17)

Why C3:C17? Because this means that we want to find the AVERAGE earnings of JANUARY

WILL SMITH	$	4,266
PAUL RUDD	$	6,855
BEN AFFLECK	$	7,728
	$	5,657

The average earnings of our 15 Hollywood stars (on January) is $5,657

STEP 4: WRITE THE FORMULA FOR CELL I3, BY FOLLOWING THE SAME STEPS 2 AND 3. Just make sure to select the correct range.

This time, you are trying to find the average for CHRIS EVANS, so the range must include from C3 to H3, and you must write the formula at cell I3.

=AVERAGE(C3:H3)

JAN	FEB	MAR	APR	MAY	JUN	
$	$	$	$	$	$	$
6,421	5,155	7,144	6,670	4,731	5,123	5,874

STEP 5: Finally, CLICK, HOLD AND DRAG THE FORMULAS.

The formula at C18 must be dragged to the right, and the formula at I3 must be dragged down.

JAN	FEB	MAR	APR	MAY	JUN	
$ 6,421	$ 5,155	$ 7,144	$ 6,670	$ 4,731	$ 5,123	$ 5,874
$ 8,750	$ 7,711	$ 6,686	$ 8,850	$ 3,862	$ 6,346	$ 7,034
$ 3,160	$ 3,952	$ 4,930	$ 3,433	$ 6,160	$ 4,736	$ 4,395
$ 3,483	$ 8,014	$ 7,096	$ 7,687	$ 7,289	$ 7,988	$ 6,926
$ 3,180	$ 5,858	$ 6,698	$ 8,090	$ 8,542	$ 7,088	$ 6,576
$ 3,679	$ 6,441	$ 3,620	$ 3,131	$ 3,122	$ 7,606	$ 4,600
$ 4,656	$ 6,059	$ 7,045	$ 7,149	$ 6,447	$ 3,404	$ 5,793
$ 3,863	$ 8,239	$ 7,838	$ 5,241	$ 6,920	$ 6,547	$ 6,441
$ 7,188	$ 3,786	$ 4,473	$ 7,603	$ 6,368	$ 8,728	$ 6,358
$ 6,920	$ 7,573	$ 6,078	$ 8,229	$ 6,288	$ 6,885	$ 6,996
$ 8,169	$ 8,127	$ 3,446	$ 8,588	$ 3,057	$ 7,002	$ 6,398
$	$	$	$	$	$	$

$ 6,530	$ 6,500	$ 4,701	$ 8,019	$ 3,292	$ 8,470	$ 6,252
$ 4,266	$ 4,698	$ 4,626	$ 8,267	$ 4,456	$ 7,464	$ 5,630
$ 6,855	$ 5,963	$ 7,120	$ 4,720	$ 3,625	$ 3,770	$ 5,342
$ 7,728	$ 5,583	$ 8,593	$ 8,464	$ 4,595	$ 3,068	$ 6,339
$ 5,657	$ 6,244	$ 6,006	$ 6,943	$ 5,250	$ 6,282	

There you have them, all the AVERAGES! Notice that it doesn't matter how many columns or rows you have, when you drag the formula, you get as many results as you need instantaneously.

Let's continue with the VLOOKUP formula!

VLOOKUP FORMULA

VLOOKUP is probably the most powerful formula for "lookups and references" and the most widely used also.

In short, VLOOKUP searches through a

complete (AND ORGANIZED) database to find what you want and writes it automatically. The only requirement is that you need to write one piece of information that relates to the information you are looking for, and write the correct VLOOKUP formula to perform that operation on your behalf.

As an example, if you have this ORGANIZED database like this (just imagine it has 1000 rows with 1000 different names, industries and companies) and you would like to create a little "ID Search tool", it would be a complete mess if you do it manually. To do that, is easier and faster with VLOOKUP.

ID	NAME	INDUSTRY	COMPANY
ID1	TOM CRUISE	Diversified Utilities	Ameren Corporation
ID2	CHRIS PRATT	Rental & Leasing Services	Aaron's Inc.
ID3	SAMUEL L. JACKSON	Packaging & Containers	Aptar Group Inc.

This one is your "Search Tool":

WRITE ID **NAME INDUSTRY COMPANY**

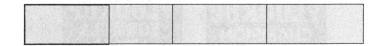

What we are trying to do is this: **Every time you write a different ID in B2, you want Excel to automatically write the NAME, the INDUSTRY and the COMPANY.** That is what VLOOKUP can do for you.

To clarify this, let's do it with an exercise. It is always better to learn through practice.

IMPORTANT NOTE:

THIS FORMULA IS A LITTLE BIT HARDER THAN THE SUM AND AVERAGE FORMULA.

IF YOU WANT TO GET DEEPER WITH THIS FORMULA, YOU CAN GET MY VLOOKUP BOOKS.

Open file ExcelBasicsChapter6ex3.xlsx

STEP 1: IDENTIFY YOUR DATA BASE, THE PLACE WHERE YOU NEED TO WRITE THE FORMULA AND THE "LOOKUP VALUE".

So, your **DATABASE** is the complete table, **from B5 to E28**.

The place where you need to write the formula is the same place where you want your result to be shown. To make it simple, let's say you just want to find the name, so the place to write the formula is **C2.**

The **lookup value** is the Variable you are going to change every time you want to get a different result. In this example, the variable is the different

ID you are going to write each time.

WRITE

ID	**NAME**

Ok, now that we have identified all those 3 things, we can move forward.

STEP 2: LEARN THE VLOOKUP STRUCTURE

Remember that the STRUCTURE of a Formula is the way you give orders to excel. If done wrong, the result would be incorrect.

=VLOOKUP(Lookup Value, Table Array**, Column, Range Lookup)**

That is the VLOOKUP STRUCTURE, let's learn it by practice.

NOTE:

Notice that each argument (part) is separated by a comma. This is important. Excel knows that you are finishing an argument when you use the

comma inside the formula.

First start writing the VLOOKUP formula by writing an equal sign, the name "VLOOKUP" and opening a parenthesis.

=VLOOKUP(

STEP 3: WRITE THE LOOKUP VALUE

WRITE

ID	NAME
ID10	CARA DELEVINGNE

The lookup value is where you are going to write "ID10" or "ID5", etc. So, the name of that cell is B2. Write B2 in the first argument, followed by a comma.

=VLOOKUP(B2,

STEP 4: WRITE THE TABLE ARRAY

The Table Array is the RANGE of the DATABASE.

That range would be from B5 to E28, and the correct way to write that range is **B5:E28**

=VLOOKUP(B2,B5:E28,

Why? Because you are ordering Excel to look inside the Database whose range its B5:E28

STEP 5: WRITE THE COLUMN INDEX NUMBER

This one is tricky. The column index number is the number of the column from which the formula will extract the result, based on the Table Array selected (Database)

In our exercise, the Table Array is B5:E28.

ID	NAME	INDUSTRY	COMPANY
ID1	TOM CRUISE	Diversified Utilities	Ameren Corporation
ID2	CHRIS PRATT	Rental & Leasing Services	Aaron's Inc.
ID3	SAMUEL L. JACKSON	Packaging & Containers	Aptar Group Inc.

B column would be column number 1 (ID)

C column would be column number 2 (NAME)

D column would be column number 3 (INDUSTRY)

E column would be column number 4 (COMPANY)

WRITE

ID   **NAME**

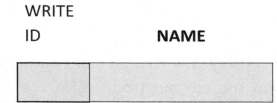

The Column Index Number would be 2. Why? Because you want to automatically **get the NAME**, and NAME is the 2nd column of you Table Array (Database)

=VLOOKUP(B2,B5:E28,2,

STEP 6: WRITE THERANGE LOOKUP

Let's make this simple, 0 is for EXACT Match and 1 for APROXIMATE Match. Try to stick with EXACT Match. To avoid having lots wrong results, so use

0 in the last argument, close the parenthesis and press Enter.

=VLOOKUP(B2,B5:E28**,2,0)**

WRITE

ID	**NAME**
ID2	CHRIS PRATT

ID	**NAME**
ID1	TOM CRUISE
ID2	CHRIS PRATT

Notice that every time you write a different ID inside B2, you will automatically get the name of the worker! That is how VLOOKUP WORKS

WRITE

ID	**NAME**
ID10	CARA DELEVINGNE

Let's continue with the last formula. The IF formula.

IF FORMULA

The IF formula is the most powerful logical formula. It is extremely flexible and can be used in numerous ways. It also can be used in conjunction with other formulas (that procedure is called "Nesting a Formula") and it is impossible to explain everything about this in this chapter.

Because of that, I have dedicated an entire book to the IF formula and I highly recommend you to get it.

My job here is to teach you how to use this

formula in record time, let's start!

Open file ExcelBasicsChapter6ex3.xlsx

In this exercise, you will find a Table with Name, Units Sold and Bonus columns. Your task is to use the IF Function to decide whether they have earned a Bonus or not.

I told you IF was a LOGICAL formula, so you need a **LOGICAL test or LOGICAL rule** to help Excel decide. In this situation, if somebody sells MORE than 59 units earns the bonus.

In the Bonus Column, **you need to order Excel to automatically show the word "YES" if the bonus was earned or "NO" if it wasn't.**

NAME	UNITS SOLD	BONUS?
TOM CRUISE	59	
CHRIS PRATT	85	
SAMUEL L. JACKSON	37	
LEONARDO DICAPRIO	71	
TOM HOLLAND	17	

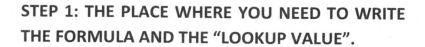

STEP 1: THE PLACE WHERE YOU NEED TO WRITE THE FORMULA AND THE "LOOKUP VALUE".

The place to write the first IF Formula is **D3**. Why? Because just like the SUM Formula, we can write one IF Formula and then drag it down to replicate that same formula throughout the table.

STEP 2: GET USED TO THE IF FORMULA STRUCTURE.

=IF(Logical Test, Value if True, Value if False**)**

The first argument (part) is the **LOGICAL TEST**: This test can be made in several ways. One of the most useful is "IF the value in a cell is greater than X number, then write X word". Another one is "If the value is equal to X, then perform X calculation".

That is the way to build "LOGICAL TESTS", they are born by the need to discern something and automate it.

The second argument (part) of the IF formula is the **VALUE IF TRUE**: If the LOGICAL TEST is TRUE, then the VALUE IF TRUE is written or calculated. This could be a Word, Phrase, Arithmetical calculation or even another Formula.

The third argument (part) of the IF formula is the **VALUE IF FALSE**: If the LOGICAL TEST is FALSE, then the VALUE IF FALSE is written or calculated. This could be also a Word, Phrase, Arithmetical calculation or even another Formula.

STEP 3: START WRITING THE FORMULA

Position yourself in D3, then start writing

=IF(

STEP 4: WRITE THE LOGICAL FORMULA

For the logical test, we need to create an argument that express "If the units sold are more than 59..."

To do that we are going to use cell names and symbols.

$$=IF(C3>59,$$

What does that mean?

- C3 is the Cell were Units Sold are
- \> is the symbol that express greater than. "If C3 is greater than.."
- 59 is the number of units sold that we stablished. "If C3 is greater than 59..."

That is the way to build the logical test (One of many possible ways).

STEP 5: WRITE THE VALUE IF TRUE ARGUMENT

Remember that the VALUE IF TRUE is the result that is displayed when the Logical Test is True. So, if the Cell C3 is greater than 59, this result will be displayed, and the result we want is **"YES"**.

$$=IF(C3>59,"YES",$$

Notice that the word "YES" is written inside QUOTATION MARKS! This is because whenever you are writing a formula and want Excel to know that you need a specific TEXT written, quotation marks are needed to distinguish that text.

STEP 6: WRITE THE VALUE IF FALSE ARGUMENT AND FINISH THE FORMULA

Remember that the VALUE IF FALSE is the result that is displayed when the Logical Test is False. So, if the Cell C3 is NOT greater than 59, this result will be displayed, and the result we want is **"NO"**.

=IF(C3>59,"YES","NO")

Again, we need to use quotation marks surrounding the NO and then we need to close the parenthesis.

NAME	UNITS SOLD	BONUS?
TOM CRUISE	59	NO

Notice how Tom Cruise didn't get the Bonus. But why? Even though the rule used 59 as the number in the logical test (**C3>59**) they need C· to be GREATER than 59, in other words, they need 60 or above.

STEP 7: DRAG THE FORMULA DOWN!

Remember to position yourself at the Bottom right of the cell with the formula, click, hold and drag down

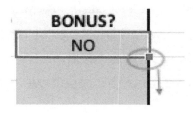

That way you'll get every single result in an instant!

NAME	UNITS SOLD	BONUS?
TOM CRUISE	59	NO
CHRIS PRATT	85	YES
SAMUEL L. JACKSON	37	NO
LEONARDO DICAPRIO	71	YES
TOM HOLLAND	17	NO

You automatically got all the "YES" and "NO" using the IF Formula!

CONGRATULATIONS! This is the end of this Chapter about the Top 4 formulas! It is time for you to continue your journey!

See you in the next Chapter!

MORE EXERCISES:

- ExcelBasicsChapter6ex5.xlsx
- ExcelBasicsChapter6ex6.xlsx
- ExcelBasicsChapter6ex7.xlsx
- ExcelBasicsChapter6ex8.xlsx

QUICK CHAPTER SUMMARY:

- Sum, Average, Vlookup and If are the Top 4 Formulas
- Formulas start with an equal sign.
- Formulas are opened and closed with parenthesis
- SUM can add any amount of numbers

- AVERAGE can do that also
- VLOOKUP finds anything inside the database
- IF creates a logical test and returns the correct result

CHAPTER 7
LEARN TO SORT AND FILTER DATABASES

It is time for you to learn how to sort and filter through databases, in order to take control of it and use it as efficiently as possible according to your needs.

BUT, WHAT EXACTLY IS A DATABASE?

A database is a set of data, formed by many rows and many columns (Lots of cells with data). Normally, they are used to record past transactions or current information.

The most important consideration to have in mind here is that the DATABASE's columns are the "Categories" while the rows are the information (data) itself. Look at the following Table.

ID	NAME	INDUSTRY	COMPANY	SALARY	BONUS
ID1	CHRIS EVANS	Diversified Utilities	Ameren Corporation	97392	5254
ID2	ROBERT DOWNEY JR	Rental & Leasing Services	Aaron's Inc.	89754	5329
ID3	JENNIFER LAWRENCE	Packaging & Containers	Aptar Group Inc.	78008	7092

Notice how you it has 6 columns: ID, NAME, INDUSTRY, COMPANY, SALARY and BONUS. Those are the categories that drive the database. Every piece of data inside that database is added according to those categories.

Also notice that the table has (in that example) 3 rows with different IDs and NAMES. Those 3 rows are part of the database. The table from above is just an example because regular databases have more than 50 rows, and in several of my books I use databases of more than 500 rows. You'll be ready to handle those databases in no time!

SO, WHAT ARE WE GOING TO DO EXACTLY?

Together we are going to explore the different choices you have to sort, filter and organize the database to find the information you want. That way, you'll have at your disposal the tools to find what you need and organize the info as you please.

Open file ExcelBasicsChapter7ex1.xlsx

You will find a database like the one at the beginning of this chapter, but larger. Your job now is to filter all the database and just show the actors whose name is CHRIS. So, let's start!

STEP 1: Start by selecting the Top Row (The categories), and you'll need to add a Filter to them.

ID	NAME	INDUSTRY	COMPANY	SALARY	BONUS

To add the filter, find this Funnel Icon at the Top of Excel (almost next to the save button) and click it.

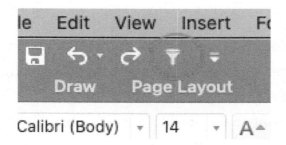

NOTE: If the button is not there, just click this button, select "More Commands" and the "Add or Remove Filters". That way you'll see the Funnel icon appear.

Now you will have those little triangle buttons facing down next to each category in the top row. That is what you are going to use to filter the database.

STEP 2: Because the purpose is to find everybody whose name is Chris, let's start filtering. Please click the "filter button" NEXT TO NAME and you will find a little window like this one

Your job is to WRITE the name "CHRIS" inside the box that I circled. And then close the window

ID	NAME	INDUSTRY
ID1	CHRIS EVANS	Diversified Utilities
ID18	CHRIS HEMSWORTH	Insurance Brokers

ID25   CHRIS PRATT   Packaging & Containers

Notice how in a matter of seconds, the table was filtered and you are only left with those actors whose name is Chris.

Also notice that to the left, where the Row numbers are shown, some numbers are not there. That is because those Rows are hidden due to the filtering process

If you want to delete the filter, just click the icon again and click "CLEAR FILTER"

That is the way to sort by writing an EXACT WORD or NAME.

Open file ExcelBasicsChapter7ex2.xlsx

The second most important way to filter and organize a database is in ASCENDING or DESCENDING order. This is what you are going to do in this exercise.

STEP 1: Start by selecting the Top Row (The categories), and you'll need to add a Filter to them.

STEP 2: Organize in an ASCENDING order by Industry. Do that by clicking the filter icon next to Industry,

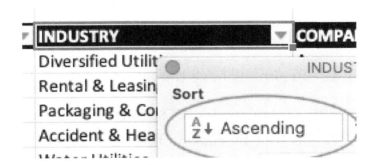

That way, you will organize the database with the Industry name that starts with "A", then "B", then "C", etc.

ID	NAME	INDUSTRY	COMPANY
ID4	CHANNING TATUM	Accident & Health Insurance	AFLAC Inc.
ID17	TOM HARDY	Accident & Health Insurance	Assurant Inc.
ID26	SAMUEL L. JACKSON	Accident & Health Insurance	AFLAC Inc.
ID32	TOM HANKS	Accident & Health Insurance	Assurant Inc.

It is that simple! But pretty useful.

Now let's try the same with the **SALARY**, but this time you are going to organize the SALARIES from the largest to the smallest. To do that, you will need to use the **DESCENDING order**!

STEP 1: You already have the filters in place

STEP 2: Organize in DESCENDING order by SALARY. Do that by clicking the filter icon next to salary and selecting DESCENDING.

NAME	INDUSTRY	COMPANY	SALARY

CHANNING TATUM	Accident & Health Insurance	AFLAC Inc.	98783
FELICITY JONES	Insurance Brokers	Aon Corp	98065
CHRIS EVANS	Diversified Utilities	Ameren Corporation	97392
SCARLETT JOHANSSON	Auto Parts	Allison Transmissio n	96868
MARGOT ROBBIE	Conglomerates	3M Corporation	95870

Notice how Channing Tatum has the biggest salary, followed by Felicity Jones.

That way you can use the ASCENDING and DESCENDING options to organize any column, whether it has words or numbers!

Open file ExcelBasicsChapter7ex3.xlsx

The third filtering option you are going to learn is advanced filtering for data with words, and you are going to learn it here with this exercise.

If you add filters and click the filter icon next to the **COMPANY COLUMN** (or any column with words) you will find an option that says **"CHOOSE ONE"**.

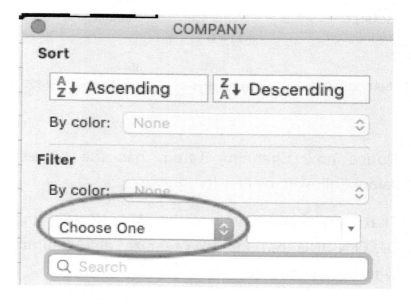

If you click it, you will find several advanced filtering options.

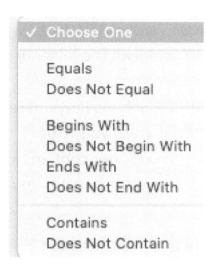

Those are very self-explanatory, but here is an overview of them:

- EQUALS: Finds the exact word or phrase you write
- DOES NOT EQUALS: Finds anything that is NOT the exact word or phrase
- BEGINS WITH: Finds whatever begins with the letter or letters you wrote
- DOES NOT BEGINS WITH: Finds whatever DOESN'T begin with the letter or letters you wrote
- ENDS WITH: Finds whatever ends with the letter or letters you wrote

- DOES NOT ENDS WITH: Finds whatever DOESN'T end with the letter or letters you wrote
- CONTAINS: Contains (anywhere in the text) the letter or word you wrote
- CONTAINS: Does not contain (anywhere in the text) the letter or word you wrote

Your task in this exercise is to filter the companies that are "Incorporated", in other words, companies whose names end with **"Inc."** (Remember to add the dot)

STEP 1: Go to "Company" column, click the filter button

STEP 2: Go to "Choose one", select "Ends With" and write "Inc."

There you go, you end up with actors who work in Companies whose names finish with **"Inc."**

ID	NAME	INDUSTRY	COMPANY
ID2	ROBERT DOWNEY JR	Rental & Leasing Services	Aaron's Inc.
ID3	JENNIFER LAWRENC E	Packaging & Containers	Aptar Group Inc.
ID4	CHANNIN G TATUM	Accident & Health Insurance	AFLAC Inc.
ID5	GEORGE CLOONEY	Water Utilities	Aqua America Inc.
ID8	RYAN REYNOLDS	Drug Manufacturers - Major	Amgen Inc.
ID9	RYAN GOSLING	Application Software	Adobe Systems Inc.
ID11	BRAD PITT	Business Software & Services	Automatic Data Processing Inc.
ID13	WILL SMITH	Consumer Services	Apple Inc.
ID17	TOM HARDY	Accident & Health Insurance	Assurant Inc.

Your second task would be to filter the companies that have the word "Auto" inside their name.

STEP 1: Go to "Company" column, click the filter button

STEP 2: Go to "Choose one", select "Contains" and write "Auto"

There you go, you end up with actors who work in Companies whose names contain the word "auto".

ID	NAME	INDUSTRY	COMPANY
ID 11	BRAD PITT	Business Software & Services	Automatic Data Processing Inc.
ID 20	DWAYNE JOHNSON	Auto Parts Stores	Advance Auto Parts Inc.
ID 23	NICOLAS CAGE	Auto Parts Stores	AutoZone Inc.
ID 40	BRADLEY COOPER	Auto Parts Stores	AutoZone Inc.

Open file ExcelBasicsChapter7ex4.xlsx

The fourth filtering option you are going to learn is advanced filtering for data with numbers!

If you add filters and click the filter icon next to the **SALARY COLUMN** (or any column with numbers) you will find an option that says **"CHOOSE ONE"**.

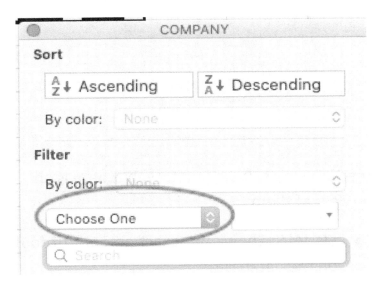

If you click it, you will find several advanced filtering options.

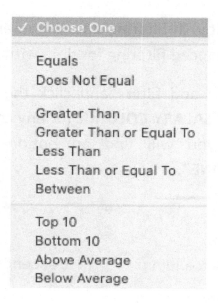

Those are very self-explanatory, but here is an overview of them:

- EQUALS: Shows the exact amount (If found on the database)
- DOES NOT EQUAL: Everything but that amount
- GREATER THAN: If you write 10, excel only shows from 11 and above (omits 10)
- GREATER THAN OR EQUAL TO: If you write 10, it shows from 10 and above
- LESS THAN: If you write 10, excel only shows from 9 and below

- LESS THAN OR EQUAL TO: If you write 10, it shows 10 and below
- BETWEEN: Shows the data between 2 numbers you pick.
- TOP 10: Shows the10 numbers that are the highest
- BOTTOM 10: Shows the 10 numbers that are the lowest
- ABOVE AVERAGE: Automatically averages and shows only the numbers that are above that average
- BELOW AVERAGE: Automatically averages and shows only the numbers that are under that average

TASK 1

Your task in this exercise is to filter the actors by salary. Just show the actors/actresses that earn a salary BETWEEN $75,000 and $80,000.

STEP 1: Go to "Salary" column, click the filter button

STEP 2: Go to "Choose one", select "Between" and write 75000 and 80000 accordingly

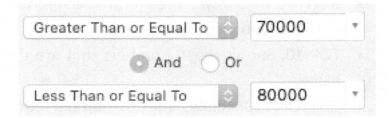

There you have your database, just 7 of them meet that criteria.

ID	NAME	SALARY	BONUS
ID3	JENNIFER LAWRENCE	78008	7092
ID5	GEORGE CLOONEY	79821	5354
ID6	JOHNNY DEPP	78171	7345
ID16	MATTHEW MCCONAUGHEY	76334	7137
ID22	EMMA STONE	78717	5308
ID34	WILL FERRELL	76066	4699
ID40	BRADLEY COOPER	76013	5345

(I deleted some columns here in the book due to space limitations)

TASK 2

Your task in this exercise is to filter the actors by BONUS. Just show the BOTTOM 10 actors/actresses regarding to Bonus earnings AND FILTER THEM ALSO IN DESCENDING ORDER

STEP 1: Go to "Bonus" column, click the filter button

STEP 2: Go to "Choose one", select "BOTTOM 10".

STEP 3: Click Descending order

ID	NAME	SALARY	BONUS
ID31	IDRIS ELBA	85831	4184
ID37	VIN DIESEL	72623	4087
ID8	RYAN REYNOLDS	93378	3903
ID15	BEN AFFLECK	74549	3537
ID35	BEN STILLER	52234	3498
ID41	AMY POEHLER	66319	3355
ID20	DWAYNE JOHNSON	81036	3318

ID9	RYAN GOSLING	66987	3207
ID11	BRAD PITT	74885	3205
ID32	TOM HANKS	69752	3057

As you may see, Tom Hanks is the one with the worst bonus. And all of them are the BOTTOM 10 regarding to Bonus.

CONGRATULATIONS! You've completed the Basic Filtering section! Now you can move forward to the Conditional Formatting and Heatmap Chapter.

QUICK CHAPTER SUMMARY:

- Basic Filtering is a great tool to organize and manage a Database
- You can filter Columns that contain words
- You can filter Columns that contain numbers
- You have several choices in both scenarios.

CHAPTER 8
CREATE BASIC CONDITIONAL FORMATTING AND HEAT MAPS

In this chapter you are going to format cells according a specific set of rules that you are going to pick, so let's start right away!

WHAT IS CONDITIONAL FORMATTING?

When you have a Database, you have the option to tell Excel "Hey, if this word appears in any cell, please fill the cell with X color" or "Hey, the amount of any cell is greater that X, please write the number with X color". That is how Conditional Formatting works.

Its main benefit is that it makes data easier to the eye by coloring and formatting cells automatically.

WHAT IS A HEATMAP?

It is similar than Conditional Formatting (because it also formats cells) but with Heatmaps you format a GROUP OF CELLS that maintain a relationship with each other, and the formatting (the color) is created according to that group of cells.

WHAT AM I GOING TO LEARN?

This topic has its own book in this series, so I highly recommend you to find more of my book. But in this chapter, you are going to learn the fast and easy way to create one type of Conditional formatting and one type of Heatmap.

Open file ExcelBasicsChapter8ex1.xlsx

When you open this spreadsheet, you'll find a similar Database to the one in the previous chapter, the only difference is that I added 1 column (Net Worth) that is going to be helpful during this Chapter and the next one.

Your task during this exercise is to "HIGHLIGHT" the salaries that are greater than $80,000. In the previous chapter you learned to filter numbers by "hiding" all other rows, but in this chapter, you are going to learn to highlight them, because normally you want to keep all other rows at sight.

STEP 1: Select the whole salary column **(from F4 to F50)** EXCLUDING the top row with the word "SALARY", you just want to select the numbers. Remember, you do that by clicking in F4, Holding and dragging the mouse to F50.

STEP 2: Now, go directly to the "Home" tab in the Ribbon and find the "CONDITIONAL FORMATING BUTTON"

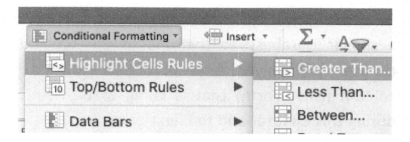

Notice that you will find several options. The one you need to click now is "HIGHLIGHT CELLS RULES" and the "GREATER THAN" because you need to highlight cells that are greater than $80,000

STEP 3: Go ahead, click Conditional Formatting, Highlight Cell Rules and then Greater than.

STEP 4: A window like this one will show up and you just need to write the value 80000 on the little empty square and click OK.

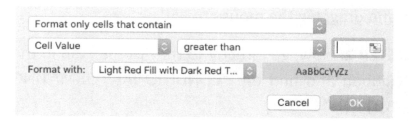

That will tell Excel that you want to highlight every single value (inside the Salary column) that is

$80,000 and higher.

STEP 5: Notice how some of the cells were highlighted and others didn't. Automatically and in a matter of seconds you got all the salaries above $80,000 highlighted, without any mistake.

SALARY
97392
89754
78008
98783
79821
78171
95870

That is a great advantage with conditional formatting. The good news is that the option "LESS THAN" (which is the counterpart of "Greater Than") works exactly the same!

Now that you have a basic knowledge of how

conditional formatting works, we can move forward to create a heat map.

Open file ExcelBasicsChapter8ex2.xlsx

This exercise is a Table with earnings divided by Quarter. Our job is to create a HEATMAP in order to visualize in an easy way all the data.

STEP 1: Select all the earnings in the spreadsheet, that is from D4 to G50

STEP 2: Go to Conditional Formatting and the select "COLOR SCALES" and click the first choice you have

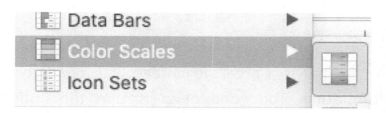

ID	NAME	Q1	Q2	Q3	Q4

ID1	CHRIS EVANS	$ 928,698	$ 1,249,879	$ 893,703	$ 1,064,963
ID2	ROBERT DOWNEY JR	$ 494,611	$ 790,880	$ 424,576	$ 1,444,624
ID3	JENNIFER LAWRENCE	$ 934,753	$ 893,295	$ 1,146,455	$ 1,060,061
ID4	CHANNING TATUM	$ 1,391,249	$ 550,366	$ 1,432,906	$ 591,002
ID5	GEORGE CLOONEY	$ 904,057	$ 799,368	$ 379,950	$ 1,138,147
ID6	JOHNNY DEPP	$ 564,675	$ 624,285	$ 1,394,050	$ 1,017,733

That's it! Look how easily you created a Heatmap that allows you to see the highest numbers and the lowest number easily all around the table.

This one is a handy tool whenever you are working with a database with several columns that are equally weighted, as an example Quarters, Months, Years, etc.

So, CONGRATULATIONS! This is the end of your basic training on Conditional Formatting and Heatmaps!

You still have to go through basic Pivot Tables training so let's go!

QUICK CHAPTER SUMMARY:

- Conditional Formatting highlights cells according to a rule that you specify
- Heatmaps do the same but using Color Scales

CHAPTER 9
CREATE BASIC CHARTS AND GRAPHS

Within this chapter you are going to create 2 different types of charts (although there are even more) and you'll familiarize with the thinking process involved to create a chart.

WHAT EXACTLY IS A CHART?

A chart is a visual representation of information. That information usually involves categories and numbers so, a chart is the best way to communicate.

WHICH IS THE MAIN PURPOSE OF A CHART?

The main objective of a chart is to **TELL A STORY!** It doesn't have to be good looking, it doesn't have to embellish the presentation, **IT MUST GIVE VALUE BY TELLING THE STORY OF THE NUMBERS!**

WHICH CHARTS ARE YOU GOING TO LEARN IN THIS BOOK?

The most used charts are the Bar Charts and the Pie Charts. Within this chapter you are going to learn how to easily create both of them and the best suitable situation for each one of them.

WHAT IS A BAR CHART?

Also known as Column charts, is a chart that has several columns (of different heights) and each column represents either a category or a specific period of time.

So, this type of chart is suitable when you

have less than 10 categories or less than 10 periods of time. This is also an option when you need to show development over time.

WHAT IS A PIE CHART?

Is a circular chart (like a cake) which shows the proportion of a whole. It is only suitable when you need to visually show the proportion each part has on the whole (100%)

So, without more introduction, let's solve some exercises!

Open file ExcelBasicsChapter9ex1.xlsx

Your job is to create a BAR CHART that shows each Quarter of Chris Evans.

STEP 1: You are going to work with the **Insert Tab** of the Ribbon and then with the groups of charts that appear there, so please locate them in your display. Go to your RIBBON, locate the INSERT TAB and the locate the little chart icons there.

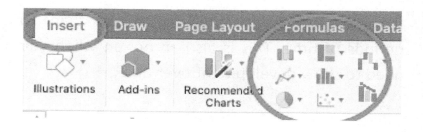

STEP 2: Now that you have located them you need to understand that there is a CORRECT way to select your data in order to get "Each quarter for Chris Evans". If you select the wrong data, you could end up with the results of Quarter 1 from each one of the Hollywood Stars.

The right way in this situation is to select the first 2 rows (The header and Chris' row) and THEN look for the BAR CHART icon.

NAME	Q1	Q2	Q3	Q4
CHRIS EVANS	$ 928,698	$ 1,249,879	$ 893,703	$ 1,064,963

So, go ahead and select from B3 to F4

STEP 3: Look for the Bar Chart Icon, click it.

Then, select the first Chart option that shows up (The 2D Clustered Column)

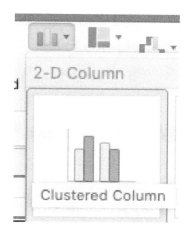

There you have it! A nice and clean Chart showing the 4 quarters of Chris Evans.

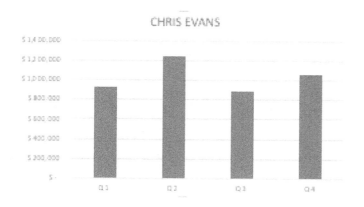

WHAT IF YOU WANT TO VISUALIZE ROBERT DOWNEY'S QUARTERS?

STEP 4: Just left click inside the chart, and you will notice little color boxes surrounding Chris Evans' Quarters. When that happens, you just need to click on any border of Chris Evans' CELL, and DRAG the selection down, in order to select Robert Downey Jr.

NAME	Q1	Q2	Q3	Q4
CHRIS EVANS	$ 928,698	$ 1,249,879	$ 893,703	$ 1,064,963
ROBERT DOWNEY JR	$ 494,611	$ 790,880	$ 424,576	$ 1,444,624
JENNIFER LAWRENCE	$ 934,753	$ 893,295	$ 1,146,455	$ 1,060,061

That way, your chart will change automatically!

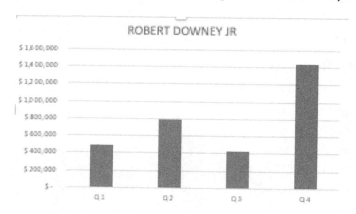

That is the fastest and easiest way to create Bar and Column Charts in Excel! It is time to create a

Pie Chart now.

Open file ExcelBasicsChapter9ex2.xlsx

Your job is to create a PIE CHART that how each Hollywood star contributes to the Overall result of the 1st quarter.

STEP 1: This step is the same as the previous exercise. Locate the chart icons.

STEP 2: The right way to select the data in this situation is to select the first 2 columns (from B3 to C10) which involve all the names and all the results for the 1st Quarter. So, go ahead and select that range.

STEP 3: Look for the Pie Chart Icon, and choose the first option.

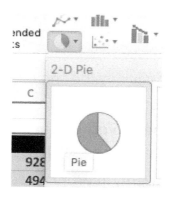

By doing that, you will automatically get the proportions in which each Hollywood star contributes to the overall result of the 1st quarter.

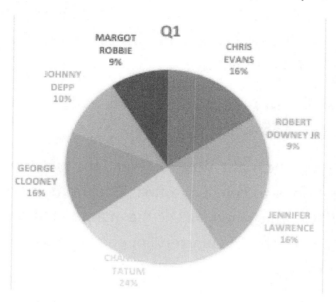

WHAT IF YOU WANT TO VISUALIZE THE 3RD QUARTER?

STEP 4: Just left click inside the chart, and you will notice little color boxes surrounding Q1 Results. When that happens, you just need to click on any border surrounding Q1 Cell (C3), and DRAG the selection to the right, in order to select Q3.

Q1		Q2		Q3		Q4
$	928,698	$	1,249,879	$	893,703	$
$	494,611	$	790,880	$	424,576	$
$	934,753	$	893,295	$	1,146,455	$
$	1,391,249	$	550,366	$	1,432,906	$
$	904,057	$	799,368	$	379,950	$
$	564,675	$	624,285	$	1,394,050	$
$	535,990	$	1,463,924	$	1,164,035	$

That way, your chart will change automatically!

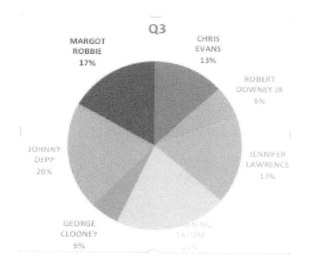

CONGRATULATIONS! Now you know the fastest way to create Charts! You just have one more chapter to go, PIVOT TABLES!

MORE EXERCISES:

- ExcelBasicsChapter9ex3.xlsx
- ExcelBasicsChapter9ex4.xlsx

QUICK CHAPTER SUMMARY:

- Charts are created to TELL a story!
- They are a visual representation of data
- The most widely used are Bar Charts and Pie Charts
- You can quickly create a chart
- You may want to grab one of my books that is completely about Charts!

CHAPTER 10
MANAGE GIANT DATABASES BY CREATING PIVOT TABLES

This is the last chapter of the book so I really want to congratulate you on coming so far. I have really saved the best tool for this final chapter.

Before starting I want you to know that Pivot Tables are not a "beginner thing". Instead, you need to really become more familiarized and comfortable with all the topics inside this book before attempting to become a Pivot Table superstar.

Nevertheless, I wanted to add this chapter at the end of the book because it serves as an introduction to Pivot Tables for you. You can also find my books that teach Pivot Tables from A to Z, those are entire books explaining just Pivot Tables! That said, let's continue.

Here you are going to learn to create powerful Pivot Tables out of a big database, and it is going to save you lots of wasted time, and, as you may know, time is money! So, you are going to end up saving money and gaining powerful insight on the data you have.

WHAT IS EXACTLY A PIVOT TABLE?

A Pivot Table is a DYNAMIC TABLE that is shaped according to your needs. In other words, you create a Pivot Table with some clicks and dragging some items, and you get to visualize the information you want, in the shape you want, ordered as you want in a matter of seconds.

The main fact here is that those "clicks and dragged items" MUST BE THE CORRECT ONES! If you screw it up and do it incorrectly, you will get a huge mess.

WHERE DOES A PIVOT TABLE COME FROM?

You have to know that a Pivot Table is created out of a DATABASE. In other words, **THE DATABASE FEEDS THE PIVOT TABLE**, always remember that.

As an example, here you have the database that we're going to be using during this chapter (obviously it is going to have more rows). Notice that is has 5 columns or categories, if you will: Name, Quarter Paid, Studio Company, Salary and Bonus.

NAME	QUARTER PAID	STUDIO COMPANY	SALARY	BONUS
CHRIS EVANS	Q1	Lions Gate	97392	5254
ROBERT DOWNEY JR	Q2	20th Century Fox	89754	5329
JENNIFER LAWRENCE	Q3	Universal Studios	78008	7092
CHANNING TATUM	Q4	Metro-Goldwyn-Mayer	98783	5437
GEORGE CLOONEY	Q3	Paramount Pictures	79821	5354

JOHNNY DEPP   Q4   Warner Bros   78171   7345

Just imagine that you are trying to solve these questions, WITHOUT Piot Tables, just using the Filters I taught you in Chapter 7:

- How much bonus was paid each Quarter?
- How much bonus was paid by each Company?
- How much was paid in Salaries in the third Quarter by Lions Gate company?

Well, you would have to take some minutes to sort, filter and perform each calculation in order to get all those answers, but using Pivot Tables you could have all the answers in less than 1 minute! (Once you have already mastered Pivot Tables, of course)

In order to answer the 1st Question "How much bonus was paid each Quarter?" your Pivot Table would look like this:

Row Labels	Sum of BONUS

Q1	43284
Q2	92146
Q3	67624
Q4	69233
Grand Total	**272287**

Notice how I created a simple nice Pivot Table, which took 20 seconds of my time to build, and I got the answer, without mistakes.

That is the awesome power a Pivot Tables!

HOW TO CREATE A PIVOT TABLE?

That is exactly what we are going to do now. Previous to start creating it, these are the requirements:

- **A Database with all the data.** Remember that the Database feeds the Pivot Table.
- **The questions you are trying to answer:** Begin with the end in mind, to do that you need to be aware of what you are trying to

discover. For the exercises, we are going to answer the 2 questions:

How much bonus was paid by each Company?

How much was paid in Salaries in the third Quarter by Lions Gate company?

That said, it is time to open your exercise files!

Open file ExcelBasicsChapter10ex1.xlsx

You will find a Database with 50 rows and 5 columns, as you were told in the first part of this chapter. Your job is to answer the following question using a Pivot Table:

How much Bonus was paid by each Company?

STEP 1: Take a look at the QUESTION and the Database, and find out which columns you are going to need in order to create the Pivot Table.

To do that, ask yourself **"Which columns of my database do I need to answer the question?"**

You'll notice that just Bonus and Companies are required to create the Pivot Table.

STEP 2: Proceed to INSERT THE PIVOT TABLE TEMPLATE.

To do that first select the whole Database (from B3 to F50). Once you have done that, go to the INSERT TAB of your Ribbon, select Tables and then Pivot Tables.

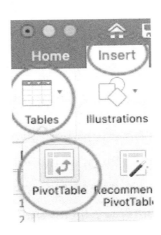

When you do that a Window will appear, basically asking you if you want your new Pivot

Table to be created on a New Worksheet, just click OK.

STEP 3: You are now in front of the Pivot Table Template and the Pivot Table Creator:

Click in this area to work with the
PivotTable report

(Pivot Table Template)

If you click on your Pivot Table Template (which is where you Pivot Table will be created) you'll notice that another field appears to the right of your display, we'll call that field the PIVOT TABLE CREATOR.

Why are we calling it that way? Because with it you will be able to shape and create the

Pivot Table the way you want it.

The Pivot Table Creator has 2 main parts: The labels and the fields where you drag the labels as needed.

PivotTable Fields

FIELD NAME

☐ NAME
☐ QUARTER PAID
☐ STUDIO COMPANY
☐ SALARY
☐ BONUS

(Labels of the Pivot Table Creator)

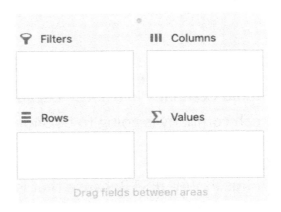

(Fields of the Pivot Table Creator)

THE TRICK IS TO DRAG THE CORRECT LABELS INTO THE CORRECT FIELDS TO CREATE THE PIVOT TABLE THAT WOULD ANSWER YOUR QUESTION!

STEP 4: Drag the correct labels in the correct fields.

Please, drag the "Studio Company" Label to the ROWS field and the "Bonus" Label to the VALUES field.

Why Studio Company in ROWS? Because that way, each company is going to be shown row by row.

Why Bonus in VALUES? Because that is the result we want to get.

Row Labels	Sum of BONUS
20th Century Fox	30308
DreamWorks	28143
Lions Gate	24504
Metro-Goldwyn-Mayer	36277
Paramount Pictures	46510
Sony Pictures	34109
Universal Studios	20974
Warner Bros	51462
Grand Total	**272287**

That is the Pivot Table you got by doing that. Notice how the total Bonus paid by each company appears next to it automatically.

That way, you can answer the question correctly and efficiently.

For the next exercise we are going to create what I call a 3 conditional Pivot Table, because it involves 3 variables (or conditionals).

Open file ExcelBasicsChapter10ex2.xlsx

You will find the same Database, but now the question we are going to answer is:

How much was paid in Salaries in the third Quarter by Lions Gate company?

STEP 1: Take a look at the QUESTION and the Database, and find out which columns you are going to need in order to create the Pivot Table. To do that, ask yourself **"Which columns of my database do I need to answer the question?"**

You'll notice that you need to include: Salaries, Quarter Paid and Companies.

STEP 2: Proceed to INSERT THE PIVOT TABLE TEMPLATE. Follow the exact same procedure than the previous exercise.

STEP 3: Click on the Pivot Table Creator to display the Pivot Table Fields. Follow the same procedure than the previous exercise.

STEP 4: Drag the correct labels in the correct fields.

Please, drag the "Studio Company" Label to the ROWS field, the "Quarter Paid" Label to the COLUMNS field and the "Salaries" Label to the VALUES field.

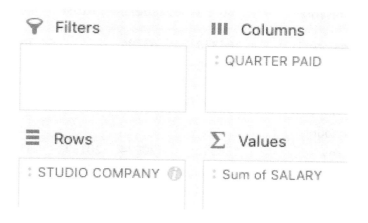

Why?

- Studio Company in ROWS because we need to display every single one of them to find Lions Gate Company

- Quarter Paid in COLUMNS because that
  way, the salary paid is going to be
  separated by quarter according to the
  actual information of the database
- Salaries in VALUES because that's the result
  we want to show.

Row Labels	Q1	Q2	Q3	Q4
20th Century Fox	76066	186622	150264	
DreamWorks	60198	220272	81036	
Lions Gate	164379	63794		74327
Metro-Goldwyn-Mayer		126127	183954	196848
Paramount Pictures	138942	170624	201321	141636
Sony Pictures	167068	163315	185802	
Universal Studios		127119	78008	90121
Warner Bros	94954	127573	69752	258723
Grand Total	701607	1185446	950137	761655

Notice how Lions Gate company didn't pay
anything as a Salary in the 3rd Quarter! That's the

power of PIVOT TABLES, you have already seen it by yourself!

CONGRATULATIONS on finishing this course! It has been a great time together and I hope you have enjoyed I and learned a lot.

Now you are ready to move forward with more advanced Excel skills. It would be great if you continued your journey by picking the next book on this series. You will be amazed when you finish the whole series and find out that now you are a Pro Excel User.

QUICK CHAPTER SUMMARY:

- Databases feed Pivot Tables
- Pivot Tables are a flexible way to summarize big databases
- Pivot Tables are used to answer important questions
- The way you use the Pivot Table Creator determines the quality of your Pivot Table

I really enjoyed being with you all this time,

and I really hope you got a great amount of value from this book. If that's the case, consider writing a review for this book where you bought it.

CHAPTER 11
LEARN WHAT MY OTHER BOOKS COULD DO FOR YOU

CONGRATULATIONS! You finished the exercises and now you are ready to continue your journey. Within this brief chapter I'm going to explain the benefits you could have by getting my other books.

EXCEL CHAMPIONS SERIES

This series is focused on delivering the most detailed information and exercises, so you can truly master each aspect of Excel. Here are some books of Excel Champions Series:

EXCEL VLOOKUP CHAMPION

Vlookup is one of the most useful Excel functions. You can use it in different ways but basically it helps you find information within a giant amount of data.

Sometimes, you need to find the exact price (or any other information) of a certain Product ID, but you have many products. What someone who is not a Vlookup Champion does is to search the price of each product in their database and copy it manually, one by one. What a waste of time! What a Vlookup Champion does is to use the formula to get the right prices from the database and in 30 seconds all the prices along with their respective Product ID are in place, with zero errors.

EXCEL PIVOT TABLE CHAMPION

A Pivot Table is absolutely one of the best tools in Excel, the benefits of knowing how to use this tool are a lot since in most cases it is almost impossible to manually perform the work done by the Pivot Table tool.

If you want to do the work manually you would spend at least 10 times more time, it is better to invest that time learning to use the Pivot Tables.

"By using a Pivot Table, the right way, you can get the answers you want in 10% of the time (or less)"

A Pivot Table is used to manage giant data tables (which we will call Source Data from now on), so you can organize the information and get the relevant answers you want.

EXCEL IF FUNCTION CHAMPION

This book was written to teach you the correct way to use the IF Functions and other logical functions quickly and easily.

It is extremely important that you know that this book is not just about the IF function, it is actually a complete guide about the main logical functions of Excel, so with this book you will also learn to use the following Excel Functions:

- IF
- IFS
- OR
- AND
- SUMIF
- SUMIFS
- COUNTIF
- COUNTIFS

EXCEL CONDITIONAL FORMATTING CHAMPION

If you have ever used graphs in Excel or Power Point you will agree that is better to present data in a visually pleasing way, so that the information is better understood.

With Conditional Format you can highlight quantitative and qualitative data automatically, which will allow you to better communicate your ideas and allow your other colleagues to understand what you are trying to communicate.

EXCEL XLOOKUP CHAMPION

To be an Excel Champion it is necessary that you master several tools and formulas. In this book I will teach you in detail and step by step the XLOOKUP formula.

The XLOOKUP feature was recently released by Microsoft to the general public in February 2020 and is here to stay.

In case you know the VLOOKUP function you will know that it is very useful. Well, XLOOKUP is more powerful than VLOOKUP.

XLOOKUP is a search formula that, if used in the right way, helps drastically reduce the time you use in front of the computer when working with databases.

The most interesting thing is that the Microsoft team managed to make it work in such a way that, in situations where we would have had to use different functions, we can now only use XLOOKUP and get the result we want.

EXCEL NINJAS SERIES

Excel Ninja Series is the fastest, the most

practice-based and definitely the most straightforward Excel Book Series you will ever find!

EXCEL FORMULAS NINJA

A Function is a formula that you can use in Microsoft Excel in order to get an automatic result based on the values that you entered in that formula. So, from now on, Functions and Formulas are the same, ok?

There are lots of different functions that perform different calculations (too many of them) so learning them all is almost impossible and not time effective because you won't use them all. So, my advice to you is the next one:

1. Learn the most useful functions first
2. Figure out which other function you need to learn in order to complete your work
3. You will find that, in most situations, the formula you need is explained in this book.

Through Excel Functions Ninja you will learn

the most useful and important functions for your work and life!

EXCEL SHORTCUTS NINJA

A SHORTCUT is a combination of key strokes (in your keyboard) that perform a specific action in your computer. They are also known as "Hotkeys" or "Keyboard Shortcuts". Normally, those actions are performed using the mouse trough the Excel spreadsheets and clicking the features in the upper part of Excel (Ribbon).

The main benefit of using Excel Shortcuts is the speed. You will notice that when you go through the exercises of this book, you will be able to work in Excel at a higher speed.

EXCEL VLOOKUP FORMULA NINJA

You will need to use Vlookup when you have a database, and try to:

- Find specific information

- Organize information based on specific criteria
- Create a Search tool
- Grab information from multiple databases at the same time
- Many other tasks related to databases

Always remember that Databases will feed your Vlookup formula. In other words, without a Database you are not able to use a Vlookup formula.

So, basically: Databases are your MAIN SOURCE OF INFORMATION, and VLOOKUP is a powerful tool that helps you to obtain the correct information FAST and EASILY! Without being you the one that spends time finding the information manually.

EXCEL CHARTS AND GRAPHS NINJA

In just a few words, a Chart is a visual representation of data. The data I'm talking about may be just a few values or a lot of them.

The main fact here is that a Chart transforms raw data into visual images that include proportions, time, variables, and some other features.

Charts transform data into images

What is even more important is the objective of those charts. Always remember that the reason you are creating a chart is to **TELL A STORY!** That's it.

The only reason to create and show a chart is to communicate the story the data is hiding. You see, when you have lots of disorganized (or even organized) numbers, it is so hard to tell if things are going the way you want or not. Even if you are a numbers maniac (like me) sometimes you may find it hard to recognize the patterns inside those numbers.

EXCEL PIVOT TABLES AND PIVOT CHARTS NINJA

This book is one of my favorite because it blends 2 of the most important features in Excel: Pivot

Tables and Charts.

Because Regular Charts are static and Pivot Tables are dynamic and flexible, instead of using regular charts we need to use Pivot Charts (more on this later)

Regarding the title of this chapter, by creative process I don't mean "innovative" but the process to "create" the desired outcome, which is, a great Pivot Chart that conveys what you want to convey exactly. Thus, following this process is science and art.

It is science because you'll need some specific steps and rules to follow through, nevertheless you'll also have the ability to move away from the rule to create your own Pivot Tables and Pivot Chart.

ABOUT THE AUTHOR

Henry E. Mejia is passionate about progress and goal achieving, he also loves to run and exercise. He works in the insurance industry and likes to invest in the stock market. While doing that, he devotes some time to create Excel written courses like this one, in order to help people to achieve their professional goals.

Henry also realized that the vast majority of people use a lot of their work time in front of the computer. That time could be used in more productive or more enjoyable activities, if only people knew how to use Excel a little better.

The goal of Henry's books is to open the door for employees and business owners to use Excel more efficiently, so they can have more and better growth opportunities, progress and free time.

Made in the USA
Middletown, DE
10 September 2024